HACKSAW RIDGE : THE TRUE STORY OF DESMOND DOSS

RONALD KRUK

Steel in the form of bullets and shrapnel rained down upon the men of the United States Army's 307th Regiment, 77th Infantry Division, as they fought their way up the Maeda Escarpment. The escarpment was an intimidating vertical rock face located on the island of Okinawa, Japan, and the soldiers who battled there during World War II affectionately called it Hacksaw Ridge.

During the war, Okinawa was a stepping-stone to mainland Japan, and more than 100,000 Japanese soldiers defended that hunk of igneous rock and uplifted coral that climbed like the Kraken above the surface of the East China Sea. On May 5, 1945, the fatigued and battered soldiers of the 307th Regiment's 1st Battalion hit the 400-foot cliff hard, hoping to shatter the resilience of the Japanese ground troops, who either nested on Hacksaw with machine guns, or moved tactically through caves that wound their way through the entrails of the escarpment, ready to ambush.

To summit the escarpment and win the island from Japan, American troops had to maneuver through a network of booby-trapped explosives, as well as mortar and artillery fire, and dodge an unrelenting barrage of gunfire. Private First Class Eugene B. Sledge of the 1st Marine Division battled the enemy on Okinawa for six weeks and called the island a "ghastly corner of hell", according to *World War II* magazine.

"Men struggled and fought and bled in an environment so degrading, I believe we had been flung into hell's own cesspool," said Sledge.

During the bloodiest battle on the Pacific, the Japanese owned the day, for the odds were too great for the Americans. The formidable enemy pushed back the men of the 77th, who attempted to ascend the cliff with human ladders or 50-foot wooden ladders, and large cargo nets. Only 48 of the 204 men who began the battle were free of injury. The soldiers who were able, retreated to safety while others lay dead and injured, shot as they climbed the stone face of the ridge, that monolith of loss that looked upon the dead, injured, and scurrying men without mercy.

However, the story of the perilous battle of the 307th did not end here. The heroics continued through a single man, who inspired the depleted American troops of Okinawa, by remaining behind with the wounded. Without protection of any sort, Private Doss, a medic assigned to the unit, looked to the heavens, said a prayer to his god, and ventured back into the shattered dusk, jogging through the rain and crumbling sludge of the muddy island, towards the enemy, to save whomever he could, as other troops in his unit followed the order to flee.

All of the fighting men on Okinawa were well-armed for protection, carrying rifles and grenades, except for Private Desmond Doss, who refused to carry a weapon of any kind on any battleground because he conscientiously objected to killing, even during a time of war.

According to Doss's account in a documentary film titled "The Contentious Objector", as he rescued soldiers one-by-one, he breathed into the air with each go-around, "Lord, please help me get one more."

The modest man of faith claims to have saved 50 wounded soldiers from certain death. His comrades claim that he saved 100. President Harry S. Truman presented him with the Congressional Medal of Honor upon his return to the United States, for his heroics on Okinawa, and the citation credits him with saving 75 lives, splitting the difference.

"From a human standpoint, I shouldn't be here to tell the story," said Doss in an interview with the *Richmond Times-Dispatch*. "No telling how many times the Lord has spared my life."

During World War II, 16,112,556 American soldiers served their country and the cause of the Allies, and only 43 received the Medal of Honor. Doss, who held a powerful allegiance to Christ, and was a devoted member of the Seventh Day Adventist Church, became the first conscientious objector to receive the U.S. military's highest honor. Today, he is one of two conscientious objectors to have received it.

PFC Carl Bentley, who served with Doss on Okinawa, said in "The Contentious Objector" that God had his hand on the young medic's shoulder.

"It's the only explanation I can give," said Bentley.

Doss was never short of spirit or conviction. It encompassed his everyday existence.

Early Years

Desmond Doss was born into an unstable America on February 7, 1919, in Lynchburg, Virginia, to poor parents, his mother Bertha E. (Oliver) Doss, a homemaker, and his father William Thomas Doss, a carpenter. During the year of his birth, worker strikes stole headlines as employees fought for higher wages and safer work environments after two years of World War I wage controls. In addition, race riots were abundant that year because of police neglect, overcrowding in urban areas, and diverse racial populations all fighting for housing, political power, and employment opportunities.

Political tensions were high as well. The anarchist bombers were creating havoc, mailing dynamite-filled bombs to prominent politicians, in an attempt to overthrow the government. These bombings provided the fuel for the Red Scare. The dark period of paranoia in American history, which politicians and the media propelled using hyperbolic rhetoric, led to illegal search and seizures, arrests and detentions without warrants, and massive deportation of suspects considered radical or anarchist in nature.

That year, legislators ratified the Eighteenth Amendment of the United States Constitution, and prohibition began soon afterwards, outlawing the manufacturing, possession, and consumption of alcohol. However, Doss's father broke the law on a daily basis.

William was an alcoholic, as firmly pulled by the liquor bottle as his mother was by the Lord. Bertha was determined in her faith, and provided the catalyst for Desmond's strong beliefs.

The film *Hacksaw Ridge*, which chronicles the life of Desmond, characterizes his father, as physically abusive, but it was not the case. The World War I veteran, who received a Silver Star for meritorious service, was more dispirited, emotionally abusive, and unavailable than anything else. However, one evening violence did infiltrate the Doss home, when his father and uncle, both inebriated, began arguing. His father grabbed a gun, and pointed it at his uncle. Before William could pull the trigger, Desmond's mother separated the two men, took the weapon, and handed it to her upset son, who went to hide it. Upon his return, Desmond saw the police carting his father away in handcuffs. As the black police wagon drove away, he swore to himself that he would never use a gun.

In the Doss home, a framed picture of the Ten Commandments was a prominent fixture. Beside each commandment, a colorful illustration interpreted each command. The picture that represented "Thou shalt not kill" was a reminder of the Bible's first murder, the killing of Abel by his brother Cain.

"How in the world could a brother do such a thing?" Desmond lamented in the book "Beyond Glory", an oral account of Medal of Honor winners. "It put horror in my heart...and I took it personally."

After eighth grade, Desmond dropped out of school to help his family with living expenses as the Great Depression took its toll on American families. The depression began in 1929, and by 1933, when Desmond was 14, the United States was falling apart. The average American family income dropped 40 percent, 15 million people (12 percent of the U.S. population) were unemployed, and half of U.S. banks had failed. Experts call the Great Depression, the worst economic downturn in the history of the industrialized world, and Doss's family was no exception to the economic suffering. The family struggled mightily, and Desmond's father tugged harder at the bottle.

Even though Desmond's public school education ended much too soon, he continued to be educated in the ways of the Lord. Through his mother's Christian teachings, the soft-spoken kid with a sweet southern accent, learned tolerance, forgiveness, compassion, and strength. Harold Doss, Desmond's brother and best friend as a child, saw him grow in mind and spirit.

"He was always helping others," said Harold in "Conscientious Objector". "He was not one to give up. He didn't know how."

In the same documentary, his sister Audrey Doss

said that Desmond helped the injured and sick whenever he could, a foreshadowing of what was to come during his military career. Audrey recalled the day that a radio bulletin announced that an automobile accident had occurred near their home. Desmond snapped into action when he heard the news that an injured motorist needed blood right away in order to survive.

"He walked three miles to the hospital and walked three miles back home after he gave blood," said Audrey.

Two days later, the hospital needed more blood for the injured woman.

"There he goes again," said a perplexed Audrey. "Walks three mile, walks three miles back."

The film "Hacksaw Ridge" fictionally shows Desmond giving the blood in order to fraternize with a nurse at the hospital, Dorothy Schutte, who would become his wife. It is not the case, however. He met Schutte at a Seventh-day Adventist church, and she did not earn her nursing degree until many years later.

Desmond was the first person that Schutte had ever kissed, according to "Faith of Doss", a website devoted to the war hero and his faith.

"He was a good Christian and I figured he would help me go to Heaven," said Dorothy.

Desmond and Dorothy became inseparable, and they would need their mutual spirituality in large amounts, during times of extended separation and near-impossible anguish, as the years carried them through life together.

Military Training for World War II

On September 1, 1939, Germany invaded Poland, stunning Polish citizens with a colossal military attack by land and air, as World War II began. Two days later, France and Great Britain declared war on Germany. From there, the war escalated rapidly over the days, weeks, and months ahead, steamrolling across Europe with shocking details of gross oppression, violence, and even genocide, but the United States of America remained mostly neutral, choosing an "America first" approach. However, the administration of President Franklin D. Roosevelt was very aware of the imminent dangers of Germany and their Axis power allies, Italy and Japan, and would not sit idle.

On September 16, 1940, the United States instituted the first peacetime draft the country had ever seen. All men between the ages of 21 and 45 were required to register for it. Desmond Doss, who was 21 at the time, registered, but his local draft board considered him ineligible because of his strict religious beliefs. In particular, the U.S. military barred Doss from the draft because of his opposition to carrying a weapon or operating weaponry, his opposition to killing any person, even on the battlefield against an opposing enemy, and his opposition to working on the Sabbath.

Draft status rejection was common before the war. In fact, the draft board sent away 20 percent of the men who registered because of "defective teeth". The U.S. military was looking for men in perfect physical health. In addition, they did not want men with philosophical or religious beliefs that might deter them from fighting without reservations. Doss received a draft classification of IAO, which made him available for "noncombatant" military service. The draft board labeled him a "conscientious objector", stating that he was exempt from military service "by reason of religious training and belief", and was assigned to "work of national importance", but would never fight on a battlefield. Initially, he followed through on that classification and immediately found a way that he could help the cause of his country, working for the Navy.

One of the precautions that the United States was taking before the war was to bolster its U.S. Naval fleet. The U.S. government set out to build battleships, aircraft carriers, and cruisers, as part of America's Emergency Shipbuilding Program. Doss began working at Newport News Shipbuilding, a 550-acre industrial plant, harbored on Hampton Roads Bay. Using carpentry skills he learned after finishing public school, he participated in the construction of the woodwork on U.S. Naval ships.

His time there would not last long, though. On December 7, 1941, a year into his work at the shipyard, Japan ambushed the United States on its own shores, decimating a fleet of U.S. Naval ships stationed in Pearl Harbor. The first wave of 183 Japanese planes devoured a quiet and beautiful Sunday morning on-and-off the shores of Oahu, Hawaii, with a ruthless attack that began five minutes before 8 a.m. Stunned U.S. sailors were sleeping, eating breakfast, or performing light duties when hell splintered the clear skies as a squadron of assault planes rose like a menacing dark cloud over the mountains, bringing with it a storm of violence.

The Japanese fighter planes killed American sailors instantaneously in their bunks or at meal tables, while other soldiers were caught below the ship as water rushed through damaged hulls and down narrow halls to drown them. The soldiers on the ship's deck, who were not hit directly by torpedoes or mounted machinegun fire, had the choice to go down with their sinking ship or jump into an ocean blazing from a fuel fire.

Fifty minutes after the first firestorm, adding additional insult and injury to the dead and dying crews of military men, a second wave of 170 Japanese planes hit the harbor causing more chaos and destruction. In all, 2,403

Americans perished into the sea; some were women and children. More than a thousand were injured. Eighteen ships were destroyed or damaged severely, along with 118 aircraft.

The surprise attack ended 90 minutes later, the United States of America joined World War II, and the people of the day became America's Greatest Generation. The entrance into the war became official the following day, during a joint session of the 77th United States Congress. An American populace and federal government, once philosophically divided over how to handle the Axis powers and World War II, became galvanized, and the U.S. Congress and President Franklin D. Roosevelt declared war on the Empire of Japan. President Roosevelt called the previous day, "a date which will live in infamy."

Thousands of men dropped everything to find a military recruiter. The U.S. military enlistment offices were full with people waiting in line for hours to enlist into the Army, Navy, and Marine Corps. Doss was no exception, joining the regular Army as fast as he could despite his "noncombatant" classification.

According to "The Reluctant Admiral", Admiral Isoroku Yamamoto, the commander-in-chief of the Japanese Navy during World War II, was cognizant of the fact that Japan had awoken a sleeping giant when they forced the United States into World War II.

"A military man can scarcely pride himself on having smitten a sleeping enemy," he said in the biography. "It is more a matter of shame, simply, for the one smitten. I would rather you made your appraisal after seeing what the enemy does, since it is certain that, anger and outraged, he will soon launch a determined counterattack."

Yamamoto had no idea just how right he would become. The United States of America was coming for Japan, and Doss would be with them. He began his regular military service on April 1, 1942. He entered the Army at Camp Lee, Virginia, and from there, the Army sent him to Fort Jackson, South Carolina, for basic and advanced training with the 77th Infantry Division.

Doss became a medic because he was not required to carry a weapon in that role, and therefore, could abide by the Sixth Commandment, "thou shalt not kill", and the Fourth, "thou shalt honor the Sabbath", which is celebrated on Saturdays in the Seventh Day Adventist church, which he still belonged. He did not consider providing aid to soldiers as a military medic to be work. His reasoning was that "Christ healed on the Sabbath", so he could as well.

Doss's fellow soldiers relentlessly harassed him during training because of his devotion to regular prayer, refusal to bear arms, and objection to working on the

Sabbath. Filmmaker Terry Benedict, who directed "The Conscientious Objector", told NPR that the soft-spoken, skinny private did not fit the Army mold of a good soldier, and therefore, his superiors and peers subjected him to relentless abuse.

"They saw him as a slacker," said Benedict," someone who shouldn't have been allowed in the Army, and somebody who was the weakest link in the chain."

Doss's commanding officer, Captain Jack Glover, tried to get him transferred because he considered him a liability. He maliciously maltreated Doss whenever the opportunity was there, but Doss defended himself when he could.

"Don't ever doubt my courage because I will be right by your side saving life while you take life," Doss told Glover, a conversation chronicled in "The Conscientious Objector".

Another officer wanted to have him discharged from the military on the grounds of mental illness. However, his superiors could not transfer, court martial, or discharge him. It was too late for that. America was now at war, and the U.S. military desperately needed soldiers, all hands on deck, with or without a weapon. Moreover, through all of the abuse and extra labor that Doss's fellow soldiers thrust upon him with outright disgust, Private Desmond Doss, U.S. Army, refused to leave his military post. He was a Christian first, but a patriot as well, and he believed in the cause of the Allied forces.

"I felt like it was an honor to serve God and country," said Doss in "The Conscientious Objector". "We were fighting for our religious liberty and freedom."

Eventually, the soldiers he served as a medic, who called him "Holy Joe" and "Holy Jesus" began to warm up to him because he was a solid health practitioner with a heart of gold, even to those who harassed him. He healed their blisters after intense marches. He treated their heat stroke and any other ill that came upon them during training. However, it was Doss's "combat" achievements that would truly set him apart and provide him with a legacy that remains today. Soon, Doss would even save Captain Glover on a faraway battlefield, winning the officer to his side.

"He was one of the bravest persons alive," said Glover in the "Conscientious Objector".

After Doss finished his training, and before the U.S. military shipped him away to parts unknown, not knowing if he would ever return home, he married Dorothy on August 17, 1942. Before he left for his first military assignment, Dorothy gave her new husband a Bible. In the book, she inscribed these words: "If we do not meet another time on this earth, we have the assurance of a happy meeting place in heaven. May God in His mercy grant us both a place there."

A difficult and daring road would now begin for "Holy Joe", by way of a cold, bitter war.

World War II on the Pacific

After Japanese squadrons obliterated U.S. Naval ships and sailors in Pearl Harbor on December 7, 1941, Japan set its sights on the American territory of Guam. The

U.S. military had a small U.S. Navy and Marine Corp garrison on the island, which numbered 271 soldiers. Most of the U.S. personnel there were not armed, and Japanese forces took the island with little effort from December 8 to December 10.

The Army assigned Doss to the 2nd Platoon, B Company, 1st Battalion, 307th Regiment of the 77th Infantry Division, and then sent him to Guam for his first tour of duty. On July 21, 1944, U.S. forces showed up to reclaim the small island of 210 square feet, which lies between the Philippine Sea on the west and the Pacific Ocean to the east. Doss and the 77th Infantry landed on July 23. On August 10, after three weeks of close and heavy fighting in the rain and dense jungles, the Japanese resistance ended there. The day after America won the battle, the Japanese commander on Guam, General Hideyoshi Obata committed suicide by disembowelment at his headquarters.

While in Guam, "Medic!" was Doss's signal to assist his fallen comrades, and he did so without fear of death. With abandon, he skirted enemy lines to treat and often retrieve the injured from harm. He was so close to the enemy at times that he could hear their whispers. Doss received a Bronze Star for his service there.

Next for Doss and his 77th Infantry division crew was the island of Leyte in the Philippines. Doss and his fellow soldiers assisted in The Battle of Leyte to reestablish sovereignty for the Filipino people after Japan conquered the Philippines in 1942. The island provided crucial sea routes for ships carrying rubber, petroleum, and other necessary wartime supplies to Japan. For more than two years, Japan occupied the Philippines until American soldiers arrived on October 17, 1944 to set its citizens free. Under the command of General Douglas MacArthur, and alongside Filipino rebels, American forces handed a swift and sound blow to the Imperial Japanese Army. By

December 26, 1944, the Japanese military had been defeated in the Philippines, assuring that Japan could not extend the war past the Pacific theater. Doss received a second Bronze Star for his service there. He had already saved many a man's life on Guam and in the Philippines, but his ultimate act of courage was yet to come.

On April 30, 1945, Adolph Hitler ended his reign as the leader of Germany, the Nazi Party, and the Third Reich, when he shot himself in a bunker 55 feet below his headquarters in Berlin. When he died, Russian troops had reached the German capital and were battling above him. In other parts of Europe, German surrender had already begun. While Europe was now free of Germany's oppressive grip, Japan continued to fight with a ferocious fervor in the

Pacific.

The day before Hitler's suicide, on April 29, 1945, the U.S. military deployed Doss's unit to Urasoe Mura in Okinawa to participate in Operation Iceberg, or the Battle of Okinawa. It was his units turn to take some punishment on the horrid island, 350 miles from mainland Japan, during an 82-day battle that would eventually claim more than 12,000 American lives.

On March 31, the U.S. Navy launched 30,000 bombs onto the coast of Okinawa to provide a safe landing spot for U.S. troops, ending a week of bombardment, and beginning the military campaign on the island. On April 1,

Easter Sunday, two divisions of the Army, the 7th and 96th, and two divisions of the Marines, the 1st and 6th, made an amphibious landing on Okinawa, becoming the first American troops to hit the Japanese stronghold, an equally important strategic post and staging ground for both American and Japanese military operations.

On April 26, the attack against Japanese troops on Hacksaw Ridge began, initiating a two-week struggle there. Doss and his division were quickly approaching the island to lend a hand in the fight on the ridge. On the way to the island, Doss penned a letter to his parents, writing to tell them that he felt his chances of returning home soon were good, but that he would not allow himself to become too confident.

"I know that overconfidence does not pay," he writes on a Sabbath morning. "If I fail to do my part in protecting life, the Lord will not help me, so I try to do my part and trust the Lord for the rest."

Everything he writes to them in the letter breathes of the presence of Christ in his life, and he hopes that God will allow him to play a part in saving at least one "soul" as he continues to help save physical, earthen-lives.

In his last paragraph, he writes to them, "This Army experience has made me stand on my own feet for Christ. I can see why the Lord saw best to separate us for a while, for this has brought me a deeper experience."

The 29th of April finally arrived for the troops of the 307th Regiment, and they immediately took over the battle at the rocky ridge after several other battalions failed to take the plateau, accumulating more than 500 casualties in the process. The troops began the assault on the escarpment only to be quickly pounded by a heavy concentration of blazing weaponry that sent the men reeling.

"Them boys fired them machine guns and things 'til the barrels was turning red," remembered V. L. Starling in "The Conscientious Objector".

First Battalion was stunned, many falling dead or wounded, while others fell back to safety. Doss remained on the field of battle with the wounded, carrying them one-by-one to the jagged cliff's edge, and then lowering each man to safe hands on a rope-supported litter that Doss had pieced and tied together, and anchored to a tree stump.

"Them guys that's wounded out there, I gotta go see about them," Doss would say, according to Starling. "That's my job."

The focused medic continued to provide aid as the days continued. On May 2, he rescued another man on the escarpment. On May 4, he treated four men whom Japanese forces gunned down eight yards from an enemy cave the American soldiers were attempting to seize. He dressed the men's wounds before evacuating each man to safety. On May 5, Doss's Sabbath, he applied dressings and administered plasma to an artillery officer as mortars fell around him, then moved him to a safe spot. Later that day, he saved another severely wounded comrade who lay helpless 25 feet from an enemy's machine gun nest.

"If they wasn't dead he'd take care of them and drag them back," said Starling. "I don't know how he kept from getting shot by the enemy."

On May 21, in the middle of a cold and wet night, Doss finally proved to be mortal during a daring attack by U.S. forces. In exposed territory, while providing aid to injured soldiers, a burst of shrapnel from a grenade pierced his leg and hip. He treated himself and remained on the battlefield for five hours until litter bearers found him. Later, doctors would remove 17 pieces of shrapnel from his leg. As the bearers carried him to safety in the midst of a tank attack, Doss's heroics continued. He spotted another injured soldier and directed his rescuers to save the other man before him. Even as blood drained from his wounds, Doss crawled off his stretcher to ensure the safety of another.

As he waited for the bearers to return, a Japanese

sniper shattered his arm with a bullet. The bullet entered his wrist, exited through his elbow, and reentered his upper arm, lodging itself there. He made a splint out of a rifle, the only time he had use for one during the war. With the bones of his arm in pieces, he finally retired to safety. He left the arena of war, too physically broken to continue, finding himself onboard the hospital ship USS Mercy, off the coast of Okinawa, that miserable island, and away from the impossible enemy fortress that took too many of his fellow soldier's lives.

On the ship, after the fog of war lifted from him for a minute, he realized something was missing. His sanctuary through all the blood and bullets, his book of religious wonder, which was given to him by his wife on their wedding day, and kept in a pocket over his heart, was gone.

"Please get word to my men," he pleaded. "I've lost my Bible."

As Doss recovered in an infirmary, United States ground forces roared up Hacksaw Ridge in one final drive to win that awful property, driving out the Japanese, and finally claiming victory over the island of Okinawa on June 21, 1945. The United States military estimates that 110,071 Japanese fighters died while defending Okinawa. After America had won the island, Doss's regiment returned to Hacksaw, one final time, to search for Doss's sentimental holy book. The miracles continued, it seemed, for his men found the Bible and mailed it to Doss's home, where it waited for his return.

Japan issued a full surrender on August 15, 1945, after the United States detonated an atomic bomb on the Japanese city of Hiroshima on August 6, and another on Nagasaki on August 9. Japan signed a formal surrender agreement on September 2, officially ending World War II.

Medal of Honor

Beside the two Bronze Stars that Doss earned during the battles in Guam and the Philippines, he received three Purple Hearts for combat injuries, and the Presidential Unit Citation given to his battalion for the men's efforts on that brutal ridge, that led to the eventual securing of the Maeda Escarpment with the assist of other units.

Moreover, on October 12, 1945, during a ceremony on the White House lawn, Doss received the Medal of Honor, the military's highest award. The citation read, in part, "Through his outstanding bravery and unflinching determination in the face of desperately dangerous conditions PFC Doss saved the lives of many soldiers. His name became a symbol throughout the 77th Infantry Division for outstanding gallantry far above and beyond the call of duty." While the powerful words were presented, President Truman shook and then held the hand of Doss.

"I'm proud of you," said Truman. "I consider this a greater honor than being the president."

Doss would spend nearly six years in hospitals, treating his battle wounds and tuberculosis. The cold and wet foxholes on those Pacific islands were determined to be the cause of the illness. Because of the tuberculosis, he had his left lung and five ribs surgically removed. The contagious ailment kept him from his son, Desmond Doss Jr. for nearly six years. After doctors no longer considered his illness contagious, he was able to see his five-years-old son for the first time. The injuries and disease left Doss 90 percent disabled. In 1976, the tuberculosis would take his hearing.

Later, he would go blind.

After doctors released Doss from the hospital, he practiced and preached his faith, mentoring children as he spoke to youth groups about spiritual character development.

In 1962, a ceremony was held to celebrate the 100th Anniversary of the establishment of the Medal of Honor by Abraham Lincoln. Doss was at the ceremony; the living recipients of the distinguished medal chose him to represent them all.

Twilight Years

Twenty years later, severe hardship would strike the family and test their faith; doctors diagnosed Doss's wife, Dorothy, with breast cancer. She suffered through it for nine years before her tragic death, but it would not be from cancer. On the way to the hospital for treatment, the Doss's vehicle rolled down a hill a mile from their home in Rising Fawn, Georgia, after Desmond lost control of the steering wheel, killing Dorothy. She died at the age of 70.

"She's the most underrated person in the whole thing," their son said, according to "Faith of Doss". "So much of what happened to my dad would not have happened had it not been for her.

While Desmond mourned, his son grew angry. "There was a gap in communication there for a while," Doss's son told the "Chinook Observer". "There came a point in time where I had to get past all that."

Doss married his second wife, Frances Duman, in 1993, and she would remain by his side until his death. In early March of 2006, Doss was hospitalized after having difficulties breathing. He returned home after he was treated, and on March 23, 2006, at his house in Piedmont, Alabama, at the age of 87, he passed away. He was buried at the National Cemetery in Chattanooga, Tennessee.

After Doss's death, in an interview with the *Chinook Observer*, his son described his father as an ordinary man that often performed in ways that were incredibly uncommon, that he operated from set of consistent principles, and that his story is one of love for his brothers, even when they did not like him much.

"The power of that is incredible," his son said of the war hero. "It's the power that distinguished the great teachers, the ability to not waver from love, compassion, acceptance, and forgiveness."

Made in the USA
San Bernardino, CA
11 December 2018